This book
belongs
to

BRYCE

I wish to acknowledge the love and support of my husband Michael for his constant encouragement and without whose presence this book would not have been possible; my son Matthew for the inspiration that ignited a spark within me; the rest of my family for their love and encouragement; and Frances Reed, cofounder of the Course In Miracles® Center in Portland, Oregon, for her suggestion that I send my drawings to Unity.—CB

Third printing 2002
A **Wee Wisdom**® Book for the Child Within Us All

To receive a catalog of all Unity publications (books, cassettes, compact discs,
and magazines) or to place an order, call the Customer Service Department:
816-969-2069 or 1-800-669-0282.

The illustrations in this book were done in black ink and colored pencil.
Designed by Gayle Revelle and Peggy Reilly

LIBRARY OF CONGRESS CATALOGING-IN-PUBLICATION DATA
Bowen, Connie. I believe in me / words and pictures by Connie Bowen. —1st ed.
p. cm.—(A Wee Wisdom book)
Summary: A collection of affirmations geared for
helping readers develop a sense of self-worth.
1. Affirmations—Juvenile literature. 2. Self-actualization
(Psychology)—Juvenile literature. (1. Self-esteem. 2. Self-acceptance.)
I. Title. II. Series. BF697.5.S47B68 1995 158'.1'083—dc20 95-19004
ISBN 0-87159-282-7
Canada BN 13252 9033 RT

Unity House feels a sacred trust to be a healing presence in the world.
By printing with biodegradable soybean ink on recycled paper, we believe we are doing our
part to be wise stewards of our Earth's resources.

I Believe in Me

Written and Illustrated by Connie Bowen

Unity House
Unity Village, Missouri

Editor's Note

One of the most important teachings in all of life is the principle of cause and effect. We always reap what we sow. When we eat nourishing food, we get healthy; when we eat junk food, we tend to get sick. Effects are put into motion by their causes.

In a similar way, the thoughts we think and the words we say are causes that shape how we experience and how we evaluate the events that occur in our lives. They may appear to be happenstance; they are not. They are effects put into motion by us.

All of us take on the royal responsibility of shaping our personal worlds. Our thoughts and words are a decree to the Universe as to what kind of life we expect. Obviously, we would be wise to think and speak carefully.

What a great gift it is to give children an understanding of the power of words and thoughts. They can build on this foundation a very good life indeed. It is also a gift to ourselves to remember the elegant simplicity of affirming and knowing the Truth about ourselves.

This is a book of affirmations. Let me remind all of us that affirmations are not true just because we say them. We say them *because* they are True! Affirmations are strong statements of Truth. They recognize that God is in us and in every situation. When we affirm, we say "Yes!" to the Truth.

This is also a book of illustrations. The silhouetted figure in each illustration represents the Divine that is within us.

We have provided pages at the back of the book so that you and/or your child or grandchild may write and create personalized illustrated affirmations. Affirmations need to be positive and expressed in the present tense. For example, affirming that you will beat your friend at one-on-one basketball may seem positive to you but it is not in the present nor is it based on Truth. You can instead affirm: *I am healthy and strong; I give my best*, for this speaks to the Truth within you.

Enjoy the playful, intriguing artwork of Connie Bowen. I appreciate how it opens my heart and stills my mind to receive the Truth of each affirmative statement. May your own inner child awake and rejoice in how wondrous you truly are.

Michael A. Maday
1995

Introduction

My son Matthew had reached his first birthday, and I had gone to the library to look for a book for him. I wanted a book that would show him what a magnificent person he was—a spiritual being capable of infinite creativity and fulfillment. I wanted him to feel his divinity and the power within him to achieve greatness.

I had only been in the library a few minutes when I had a strong feeling that I wouldn't find what I was looking for among the shelves.

When I returned home, I immediately started sketching some ideas I had about love, about our true Self.

It wasn't until a few months later that I realized what I really wanted to do was to write out some affirmations, then illustrate them in a way that would be appealing to children and to the inner child in us all.

I took about a week off from my busy court reporting business and wrote out fifty affirmations and began to illustrate them with colored pencil. It was as if I had opened the door just a crack by my willingness to serve God in this way, and the Universe was now widening this open door. The more I drew, the more ideas and images kept coming to me.

I found my best time to draw was from 9 p.m. on into the night when Matthew was asleep and the house was quiet. The time slipped by unnoticed as I felt compelled to keep drawing. I would glance at the clock, and it would be 10 p.m.; then what seemed like twenty minutes later, I would glance at it again, and it was 1:30 in the morning.

It has now been two years, and I see the fulfillment of my dream—a book to use as a tool to realize our inner greatness, our immense potential to achieve our cherished longings.

Through positive images and positive statements of affirmation, we focus our energies in a productive way, turning from false appearances to the infinite Good that is our birthright as children of the Spirit of Love.

I dedicate this book to all who seek to know themselves. May you find in its pages the glory and the beauty that are you.

Connie Bowen
Lake Oswego, Oregon
1995

I am wonderfully creative.

I am safe.

I give with joy.

I learn and discover
new things every day.

I am powerful.

I am free to be me.

I am helpful and caring.

I have a place of stillness
within me.

I follow my heart.

I make friends easily.

I am thankful.

I share my love and
watch it grow.

I am forgiving.

I believe in me.

My dreams are coming true.

I am kind to others, and
they are kind to me.

I turn within,
and I am at peace.

I am filled with greatness.

I enjoy new experiences.

I am healthy and strong.

I am whole and perfect
just the way I am.

I am one with all life.

I am loving.

Laughter and joy fill my heart.

I love and care for myself.

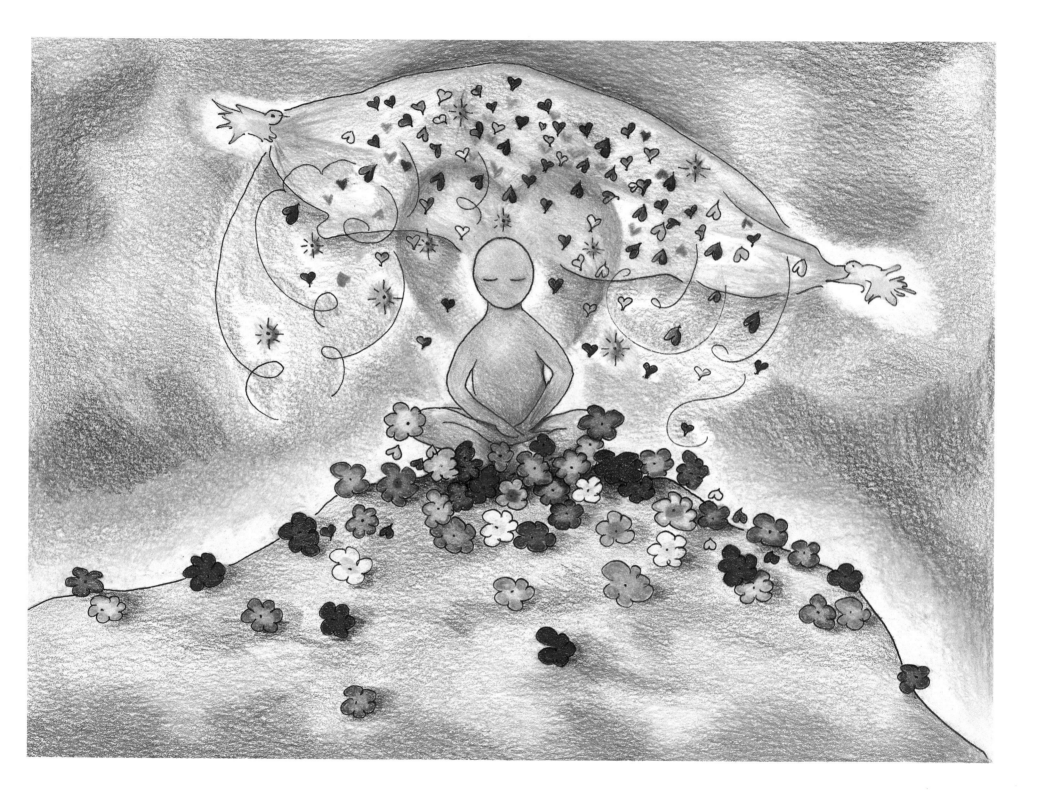

I am blessed.

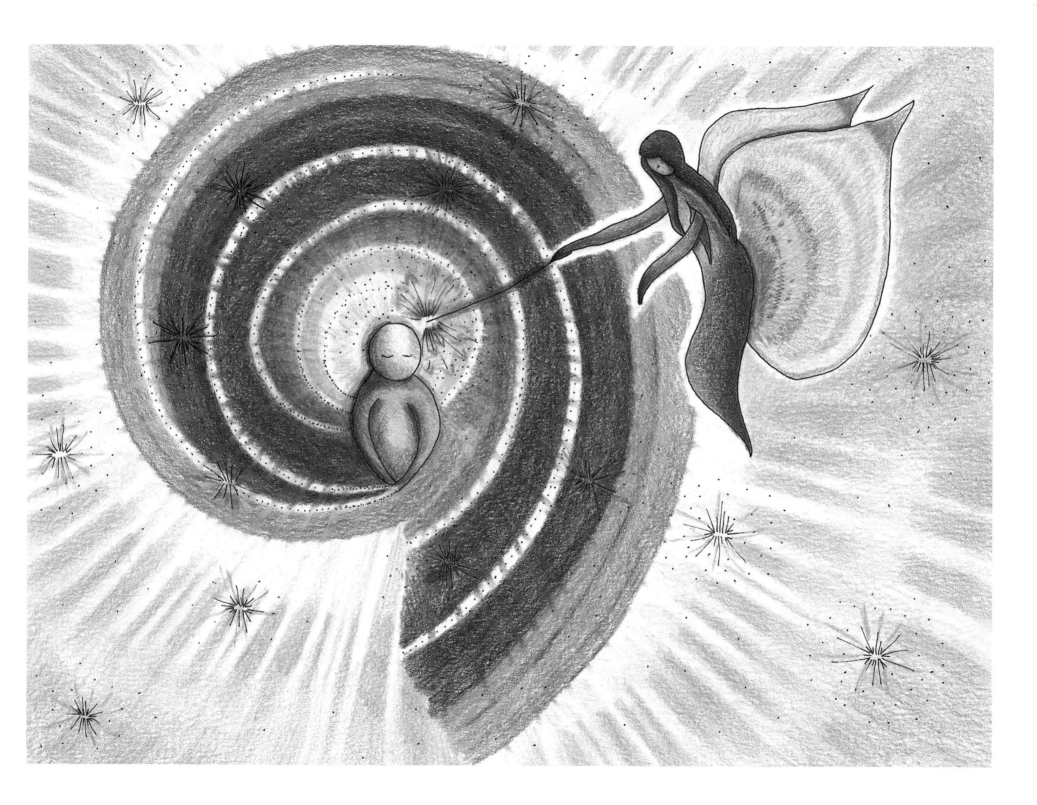

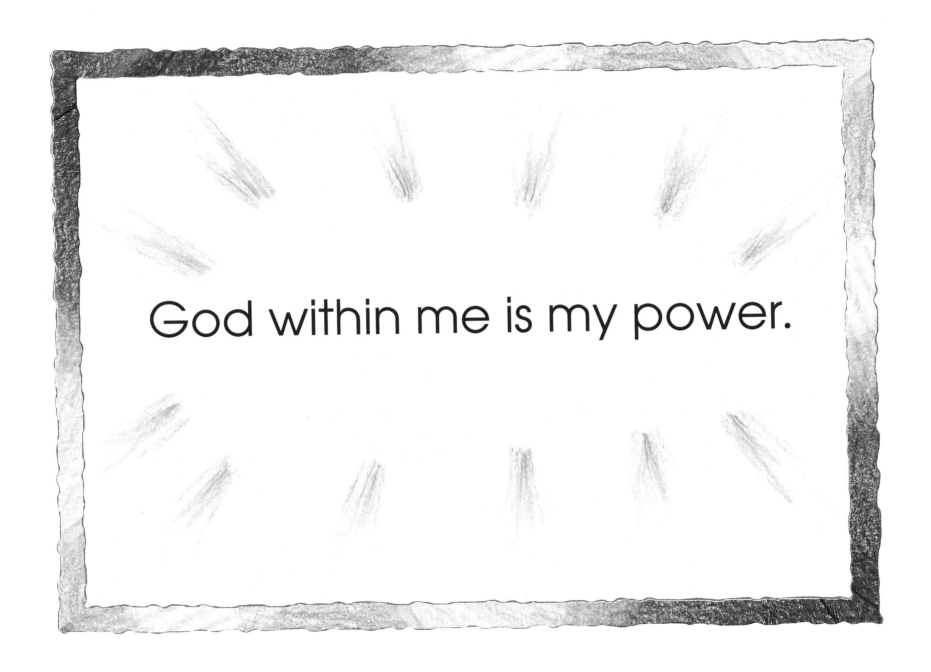

God within me is my power.

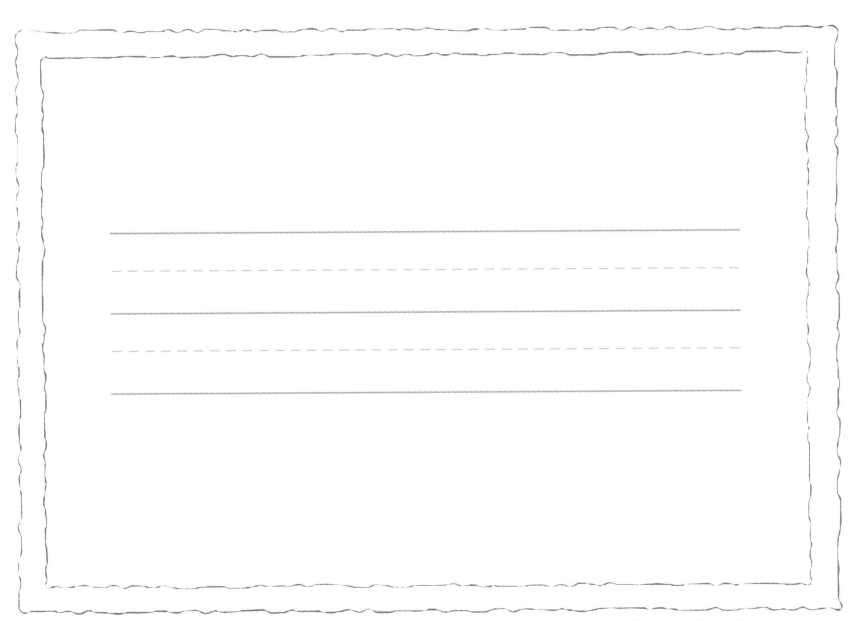

Write and draw your own illustrated affirmations on the following pages. Please refer to the Editor's Note at the beginning of this book.

About the Author

Connie Bowen has always loved to draw, and she majored in art at Washington State University. She works in colored pencil combined with pen and ink. *I Believe in Me* was her first children's book. Inspired by her son Matthew, the book won the national Athena Award for Excellence in Mentoring. It is available in Spanish as *Yo Creo en Mi*. Connie also wrote and illustrated *I Turn to the Light: A Book of Healing Affirmations*, and she provided illustrations for *The Sunbeam and the Wave* by Harriet Hamilton. Connie and her husband Mike and son live in Portland, Oregon.

Visit Connie on-line at <www.conniebowen.com>.

Printed in the U.S.A.

174-0657-7.5M-3-02